1

ABUSER'S

DAUGHTER

ISBN: 0-9778155-0-1

Printed in the United States by Morris Publishing
3212 East Highway 30
Kearney, NE 68847
1-800-650-7888

Additional copies of this book are available by mail.
Send $15.50 each (includes tax and postage) to:
HATCHBACK Publishing
Mailing Form in the back of book

CONTENTS

Dedication

This book is dedicated to my husband who watched me, prayed for me, encouraged me, supported me and loved me throughout the completion this book.

This book is dedicated to my daughter. You are the joy of my life. This is for you and your future children so that the weapon of truth will always be available. The gospel of Jesus Christ is your way to all truth. In Him alone we have salvation. May your life always reflect the love and grace of God.

This book is dedicated to every adult who has experienced trauma as a child. May you always find a place in the grace of God.

Acknowledgements

It took many other people to help me with this book. I want to thank them for taking time out of their lives to give me insight and wisdom.

Thanks Writer's Group.

Thanks Stephanie.

Thanks McKinley.

Thanks Sandra.

Thanks Tracy.

Thank You God, for strengthening me and allowing this project to come to pass.

Prologue

There was a time in my life, I thought all of the things that were happening in my family was normal. Everybody's family has some sort of secret, right?

I am the daughter of the abuser who tells this story. I have a perspective that is a little different from the one's who have been physically abused.

I knew about some of them. I suspected a few more. With some, I had absolutely no idea.

Trying to be normal in a family where abnormal is the standard.

Why didn't he touch me? Was there something wrong with me?

This story is written to equip us with the weapon of truth to be set free of those memories that may still come to torment our minds from time to time.

In the Beginning

Dear Journal,

Another day has come to an end and I can say that God's grace is sufficient for me.

My husband, Bernie is already asleep and I just kissed my precious daughter Clarise good-night. Now I can finally have my quiet time before I go to bed. I truly have to thank the Lord for just how good He is to me.

My life is good now. I have a wonderful God-fearing husband and a beautiful daughter.

Things have not always been this way. God has brought me through some trying times.....

When I look back over my life, the earliest I can remember is my first day of kindergarten. I was excited. Momma used her new Polaroid camera to take a picture of my cousin Tanya and me.

After our pictures, Momma walked us to our classes. Tanya's classroom was across the hall from mine. Momma pulled me close to her and held on tight before she said goodbye. It felt good in her arms. She was so soft.

Some of the children were crying but I felt glad to be away from home. There was always so much fussing going on at my house.

School seemed like the best place in the world. We lay on towels and the teacher, Miss Stewart, read us stories. My favorite was Cinderella. I was in the morning class and at the end of the day, we stood in line and each of us got a graham cracker. When it was time to go, Momma would be right outside of the door.

Daddy was not home when we got there. He worked first shift in the GM factory where they make cars. I called him Daddy but Momma called him Donny. He would be home soon and Momma would go to her job at the big hospital where I was born. She takes care of the newborn babies.

Momma's name was Sarah and she had a big family with lots of sisters. I was her only child. I asked her why I didn't have brothers and sisters.

"I tried to have another baby," she said as she rolled her hands in her lap, "But I couldn't, the doctor told me not to try no more."

I felt sad for Momma and for me. Having someone else to play with would be a lot of fun.

Momma allowed her sister, Aunt Tammy to baby sit me while she went to work. She was mean. She chased me around the house with hair out of a comb and yelled, " King Kong, King Kong!" I hated her. I would cry sometimes and tell my parents, but they seemed not to care. Momma would tell her to stop it, but she didn't.

****

It wasn't long before I heard Daddy's car pulling into the driveway.

"Hi Daddy," I giggled jumping into his arms when he came in.

"Hey, how's my baby?"

"I'm fine."

He gave me a dollar and I put it in the secret place in the back of the clothes closet
in my bedroom.

When Daddy came home I felt it would be a good time for Aunt Tammy to leave, but she didn't. She warmed up our dinner Momma cooked before she went to work.

"Clare."

Aunt Tammy was calling me to come and eat. We all sat for dinner with Daddy sitting at the head of the table. I ate slow because I didn't like chewing food. It seemed to take so long for it to get small enough for me to swallow without choking. I hate to choke.

"You eat just like a bird," Aunt Tammy groaned with a sneer on her face.

Daddy added, " Eat all of that food so you can put some meat on your bones."

"*How can eatin' rice put meat on my bones?*" I wondered to myself as they left the kitchen and went into the living room.

I heard them sit down on the furniture. Momma put hard plastic on all of the chairs
so we wouldn't get them dirty.

When I finished my dinner, I went into the hallway that faced the living room. Daddy was sitting in his favorite green chair by the front door reading the newspaper. Aunt Tammy was sitting on the couch across from him.

"I'm done," I sang.

I noticed Aunt Tammy was sitting with her legs opened with no underwear on, so Daddy could see between her legs. She closed them in a hurry when she heard my voice. I knew this was not right and it made my insides feel funny, so I pretended not to see it.

"Come on in, I'm gonna tickle you," Aunt Tammy said.

She pulled me to the floor and held me on my stomach. I
could feel her lifting up her skirt so Daddy could see.

This ain't right. I wanna get up!

"Let me go!" I shouted .

It took a while but she let me go. I went outside to play.

*I hate being in the house with them. Why doesn't she go
home? I wanna tell Momma
but I'm afraid Daddy would get mad at me.*

I went to the garage and got my bicycle. It was red with
training wheels and a basket. I rode up and down the sidewalk as
fast as I could to the corner of the block.

"Sazell, Sazell!"

I heard Daddy calling me. His voice was loud. Sometimes he
called me that, I didn't know why but I knew it was time to take
Aunt Tammy home.

I took my time riding home. I pushed one peddle all the way
down, then another peddle all the way down. I didn't want to be
around them anymore. It made me feel funny.

After dropping her off we went to Aunt Rachel's house.
Daddy and I often visited Aunt Rachel and her children. They
were older than me but I had someone to play with.

When we got there, Daddy gave us money to go to the store. I felt so grown up walking to the store with my cousins. I was excited to buy those pink sugary graham crackers for a dime.

My parents bought me a pair of PF Flyer tennis shoes. I saw on the television where these shoes made you run faster and jump higher. I ran and jumped all the way to the store.

On our way back, I ran all the way. I wanted to prove to them, these shoes made me run faster. When I got to the house, I went through the front door and into Aunt Rachel's bedroom. She was on her bed wearing a see through night gown. Her legs were opened and she had no underwear on. Daddy was sitting across the room from her in a chair. Aunt Rachel's eyes opened big. I surprised her.

"Get out!", Daddy hollered with a frown I had seen before. His eyes were dark. It looked like his eyebrows were touching just above his nose.

I ran out of the room, scared and shaking. All I wanted to do was to show him how fast I could run in my new shoes. I got that funny feeling in my stomach again. I could not say anything to Daddy about what I just saw. I knew that my Momma would not like what he was doing. I went outside and sat on the porch.

Why is Aunt Tammy and Aunt Rachel being naked in front of my Daddy. Don't they know they should have clothes on?

I ate my cookies as I watched cousin Tony snatch the bag of

potato chips away from his brother Larry. Larry chased Tony down the street toward the house.

"Y'all play too much," grumbled Samantha. She was older than the both of them. She took her time walking down the street. She acted like she was the boss of everybody.

"Gimme me back my chips!" yelled Larry.

" Here, take 'em." Tony pushed them back into his older brother's hand.

Daddy came out of the house onto the porch. "I'll give y'all some money if you wash my car."

The excitement about getting more money made us go to work right away.

Daddy always had nice cars. This one was a white Buick with a black hood and black on the inside.

Tony got the water hose from the side of the house while Samantha and Larry found some rags.

"Clare, you clean the inside of the car," said Samantha.

There she goes again always telling somebody what to do.

Without a word, I jumped inside of the car to straighten it out. As I was picking up the gum wrappers and other small pieces of trash from the floor, I noticed something sticking out under the floor mat. I picked the floor mat up to find it wasn't paper at all. In my hand I held a black and white picture from a camera. On this picture was my Aunt Sue, another one of

Momma's sisters. She was sitting on top of a cedar trunk and she was naked. Immediately my stomach began to hurt. I hurried and put the picture back before the others could see what I had. Once again, I pretended not to know anything but my insides were yelling, " *Tell Momma, tell everybody.* "

Soon after we finished cleaning the car, Daddy and I went home.

When we got there I was surprised to see Momma's car in the driveway. I jumped out of the car and ran into the house. She was sitting in her favorite spot at the kitchen table.

I wanted to scream, "*Momma I got something to tell you. Guess what I found in Daddy's car? And that ain't all Momma, guess what I saw them doing?* "

But I didn't say any of that. I was too scared. *What would Daddy do if he knew I told?*

My Daddy was a big man and very tall. He had a loud and strong voice that made me shake on the inside when he spoke. I knew that he would be very mad at me but I felt like Momma should know.

I whispered to her as I stood by the refrigerator, "Momma when I get older I have something to tell you."

I went to my bedroom. I heard my parents talking. It was time for bed.

****

The next morning after school, Momma and I went to the store in Daddy's Buick. As we pulled back into the driveway, Momma noticed the picture on the floor of the car.

Oh no, I didn't put the picture all the way back under the mat. My insides started

shaking.

"What's this?" she questioned as she picked it up.

I knew that she wouldn't like it. I saw the look on her face as tears filled her eyes. I knew what she was looking at. I was mad at myself for not putting that picture all the way under the mat. I was mad at Daddy for making Momma cry.

Momma, that's what I've been trying to tell you. I knew all of the time.

I got out of the car and went into the house without saying a word. Momma came in,

laid the picture on the table and began to put the groceries away. I took a peak at it.

Yep, that's the same one.

Momma saw me. " I'm gonna talk to your Daddy when he gets home from work."

I didn't feel like a little kid. I felt older on the inside. I knew things that my friends didn't know. I knew that if Momma said anything to Daddy about this my family could break up. I tried to make her feel better.

"If you wanna leave I'll go with you," I said. I gave her a hug and went into my bedroom. I was scared. I was very scared.

What was my Daddy going to say? What was he going to do?

Daddy had a second job as a Security Officer at a bowling alley and he carried a gun. He had a different gun on the top shelf of Momma's closet. I didn't want to hear them arguing. I didn't want to see them fight. I didn't want to see him hit her again.

It seemed like the day went by slow. It started to get dark outside and Momma turned on the lights in the house. I heard Daddy's car pull in the driveway and open the back door. Any other time I would run and give him a hug, but not tonight. Little by little I came out of my bedroom and stood at the kitchen door.

" Look what I found," Momma announced pointing to the picture. Her voice was shaking and I thought she was going to cry again.

Oh no, he is going to start cussing and yelling.

Daddy picked up the picture. He stated in a very calm voice, "So."

I couldn't believe it. He was acting as if it was no big deal.

" I found this picture in *your* car!"

" It's not mine," he insisted.

" I'm gonna take this picture and go talk to a lawyer," she threatened.

He suggested with a half smile on his face, " I'll tell 'hem the picture belongs to Ray."

He was talking about my Uncle Ray. He was Aunt Mary's husband who was Momma's youngest sister. I didn't even know about this one.

He went into their bedroom and Momma began to cry again. I went to my room. The house was very quiet.

I didn't understand. *What was Daddy saying, that Uncle Ray was in on this too?*

At times like these I wished for a brother or sister, someone to be here with me so that I wouldn't have to live like this alone.

The next day came and so did the next. I never heard Momma mention the picture again.

I was confused. *Didn't they know that this was wrong?*

We went to church every Sunday. Daddy was the Sunday School Superintendent
and on the Deacon Board. Momma sang in the church choir. My Aunts also went to the same church and worked on the Nurses' Board. We took family vacations every year.

Will somebody please tell me, will somebody please just say out loud that this is not how a family is supposed to be?

A Change Has Come

Everyday was not a bad. I went to school, played with friends and did all the things
I liked. But there was always that chance of me seeing or hearing something that I had to pretend was not happening.

For awhile Momma worked the early shift at the hospital. I would sometimes wake up with my parents early in the morning. I could smell the coffee. I loved the smell of toast and eggs Daddy cooked before they left for work.

"Well, look who's up," Daddy said while scrambling the eggs.

"Hi baby." Momma gave me one of her soft hugs.

Heading for a chair at the kitchen table I wiped the sleepy out of my eyes. "Good morning, what time is it?"

"It's only 5:00 o'clock," Daddy responded as he sat down.

I watched him as he put the other sugar in his coffee. Daddy had something he called
"sugar." He had to take shots and he could not use the regular sugar.

"Can I have a cup of coffee Momma?"

Momma put coffee, sugar and a lot of milk in a cup and gave me a saucer to put under it. I felt so grown up sitting at the table with Daddy drinking coffee.

Daddy finished his breakfast and put everything in the sink.

He made his lunch and put it in a tin black box.

"I'm going to get Tammy." He headed toward the back door.

" Bye Daddy."

" Bye baby, you be good now, ya hear?"

" Come on now, it's time for you to go back to bed," Momma coaxed as she put the cup and saucer in the sink.

****

Daddy called during the day to talk to me. After we hung up the telephone rung again.

" Hello," I answered.

"Tammy, please."

This strange man was asking to speak to Aunt Tammy. I knew I had heard this voice before.

"Hello?" I asked again so that I could hear it.

"Tammy, please."

Oh this is my Daddy. He is trying to change his voice to fool me. I wanted to say
"Daddy, I know this is you," but I thought I better not.

"Aunt Tammy, telephone."

She was in the living room watching television. She got up and went into my parents bedroom and picked up the other phone.

"I got it. You can hang up now," she said as she sat on my parents bed.

I went a little way into the living room but I stopped so that I could hear what she was saying. I couldn't make out any words because she was whispering.

Why is she in my parents bedroom whispering to my Daddy on the phone? This is not right. I don't like her.

After awhile, Aunt Tammy hung up the telephone. I ran and sat on the floor in front of the television.

As soon as she sat down, I turned around and asked, "Who was that man on the phone?"

She said with a smile on her face, "That was my boyfriend. His name is Jimmie Lane."

I knew that she wasn't telling the truth. *Why was she saying that my Daddy was her boyfriend?*

I went outside to play.

Each time the telephone rang and the strange man was on the other end, I knew that it was Daddy. Once again, I pretended that what was happening, really wasn't.

****

When I was ten years old, Momma returned to work in the afternoons. I missed her not being at home. Aunt Tammy was there more often. She combed my hair. She fixed my dinner. She seemed to be taking Momma's place.

One beautiful summer day, Daddy came home from work and not too long after, Aunt Rachel came over. It must have been her day off work, because she goes in the afternoon with Momma.

I heard Daddy calling me from inside of the house, "Clare, come here."

I ran from the backyard and came in.

"Yes Daddy?

He went into his pocket. Daddy always kept a lot of money in his wallet.

"I want you to go to the Kressage store and buy yourself a new ball."

"Thank you Daddy." I hugged his neck and ran out of the door.

I told my friends, Sherrie and Carla, Daddy had gave me some money and we all walked to the store together.

When I arrived back home, I didn't go in the house. We began to play dodge ball in the backyard.

"You're out!" Sherrie jumped up and down and screamed. I could tell she was happy. I was mad.

It was a hot day and I wanted something to drink. I decided to go into the house and get a cold glass of milk. I got to the back door and the screen door was locked. I knocked on the door and Aunt Tammy came and held the screen door so I couldn't get in.

"Let go of the door, I wanna get something to drink."

She glared at me and didn't say a word, while holding on to

the door.

I began to feel angry inside. I didn't want to play with her. I wanted some milk.

"Where's my Daddy?" I asked.

"Go back and play," she snapped in that I can tell you what to do voice.

By this time I was really mad. I wanted to kick the bottom of the screen door so that it would make a lot of noise. I wanted to kick her. This was not her house. I wanted some milk. I wanted my Daddy. Then I realized something, Daddy was in the house and so was Aunt Rachel. *Something was going on.* I didn't know exactly what but I knew that I might as well forget about the milk. I wanted to bang on the back door and holler for Daddy but I knew that he would get mad at me. So instead, I went back to play, hot and sweaty, pretending not to know *something* was going on in my house.

****

Momma and Aunt Rachel worked together taking care of the babies. When Aunt Rachel went to work she dropped her children off at our house. I think she became afraid after Larry's drowning accident. Daddy took them back home one hour before their mother got off work.

Tony was two years older than me and Samantha was four years older. When Samantha came, she liked to sit in my bedroom. I had a television and a teenage telephone with a separate line. Momma said that she was tired of me tying up her phone, so Daddy decided it was time for me to have my own phone.

One day Daddy told me and Tony to ride our bikes and drop off flyers. He had taken an interest in who was running for the City Council.

"Samantha are you going?" I asked.

" Naw, y'all go ahead," she answered with her head down.

Tony and I went outside and got on our bikes.

"Maybe she thinks she's too grown to go," Tony pointed out. He shuffled the flyers under his arm and rode down the street.

I rode my bike up the hill in the opposite direction. I went for two blocks going door to door putting flyers in mailboxes or sticking them inside of the screen door. I handed out quite a few flyers but it was a real hot day and I was thirsty. *Who cares about who wins City Council anyway? I want some milk.* With the few flyers I had left, I decided to go home, get some milk and start over again.

When I got there, I took my sandals and placed them on the steps next to Samantha's.

Momma didn't like it when we wore our shoes in the house. She said it got her floors

dirty.

I went to the bedroom to see what Samantha was doing. When I made it to the hallway, I could see Daddy laying on top of her on my bed. They both had their clothes on. I was scared! I didn't want to go in the room so I hurried back into the kitchen and slammed a cupboard door so they would know I was in the house. I heard the bathroom door close. Daddy walked into the kitchen, straightening out his clothes.

"Where's Samantha?" I questioned.

He spoke without taking an extra breath, "Across the street at Jamie's house."

Maybe I was just imagining. Maybe I really didn't see them. Maybe the sun was so hot on my head outside that I really didn't see what I thought I saw. Maybe I didn't hear the bathroom door close.

Daddy walked into his bedroom. I got some milk and decided to go hand out the rest of the flyers. I went to the steps to put on my sandals and there was Samantha's shoes. I knew that she would never go outside without her shoes. She was too *grown* for that too. She definitely wouldn't go to a neighbor's house without them.

My stomach started hurting. I felt like throwing up. My hands were shaking as I picked up the flyers and got back on my bike. I was confused. *He never touched me. What was wrong with me? I knew that I was skinny and my breast hadn't started to grow yet, but didn't he love me? I was his only daughter.*

I walked up the sidewalk to the next house and then something inside of me changed. I stood there frozen. Tears started burning down my cheeks. *I didn't want him to touch me! I believed Samantha didn't want him to touch her either! Why didn't she tell somebody? Why didn't she tell her mother?*

I ran to my bike and rode as fast as I could to the nearby park. The tears were coming down so hard that I could hardly see. I realized that Samantha could not tell her mother. Aunt Rachel was mixed up with my Daddy too. Samantha was trapped! I thought about telling Momma but I remembered the picture of Aunt Sue. She wasn't gonna do anything.

I sat in the park for awhile until late evening. I thought about that Sunday a few years ago on Mother's Day. My neighbor Jamie put plastic flowers in jars with water in it for our mothers. I woke up early that Sunday excited about giving Momma her present. I heard Momma's voice.

" Please don't hit me Donny, *please!"*

I ran to the kitchen and Momma was laying on her back with Daddy on top hitting
her with his fist.

"Stop it Daddy, Stop it!" I screamed.

He stopped and gazed at me. He looked like a bull that was getting ready to charge. He was puffing and out of breath. He got up and went to his closet and began to get ready for church. Momma got up and went into the bathroom. I heard water running and her crying. I ran back to my bedroom, shaking and terrified.

Daddy came into my room.

"What's wrong with you?" he asked as if he didn't know.

"Nothin' " I lied. I was too afraid to tell the truth.

"Get ready for Sunday School. We don't want to be late." He turned on his heels and left.

I saw the brown paper bag that I had put her gift in. It was Sunday *and* it was Mother's Day and he had ruined it. Momma didn't come to church that Sunday. She had to wear sun shades for awhile after that because she had a black eye.

No, Momma wasn't gonna do anything. I made up my mind. If he *ever* touched me, I was gonna tell everybody. That was it. I was afraid of Daddy but I wasn't going to let him touch me.

As I dried my tears, I got on my bike and headed for home. I knew that pretending that these things weren't happening was over. *How could they tell me what to do or how to act? What were we going to church for? I thought Jesus was supposed to make all things better?* My family was acting one way on the outside of our house but we were another thing on the inside.

I didn't know what I was going to do. All I knew was that I had changed. I had a feeling on the inside of me that seemed to take over. I hated my Daddy and my Momma. I knew that I couldn't show it. I was too afraid. But a change had come.

Still Going On

Aunt Paula, Tanya's mother, lived one block away from our house. She was married and had two other children besides Tanya. Roy was older than me and her other son Matthew was younger. Aunt Paula didn't let anybody mess with her, she was always telling somebody off. Momma and I visited her a lot.

One summer afternoon, while riding my bike, I decided to go to their house.

"Hey is anybody home?" I hollered as I walked in the back door.

I heard an answer from upstairs. "I'm up here. Come on up!"

It was Roy. He was the only one home. I ran up the steps to his bedroom. I liked him a lot. Even though he was seven years older, he never acted like he didn't have time for me. He always kept his things so neat and clean. Even his penmanship was neat.

"Whatcha' doin?" I asked as I sat on the end of his bed.

"What does it *look* like I'm doin?" he joked with a grin.

"Cleanin' up this mess I hope."

I looked around his bedroom. He had pulled two of his drawers out of the dresser and was at the other end of the room carefully folding and separating his shirts. The other dresser drawers were opened waiting to be sorted.

"What are you doin' today, just ridin' your bike?"

"Yep, there's nothing else to do."

I softly bounced on the end of the bed to the music that was playing on the radio. I noticed a brown covered notebook in one of his opened drawers. I picked it up and began to read it. I noticed Daddy's name and I turned back a page to get a better look.

Roy had written in his journal that he was having sex with Aunt Tammy and Aunt Rachel. They were at Aunt Tammy's house on her bed. Daddy was there in the room, sitting in a chair. Roy wrote that he felt like my Daddy liked to watch them. I couldn't believe it. I looked at Roy in disbelief and he saw me with his book. My heart began to pound really fast.

"Put that back!" he insisted with a voice mixed with anger and surprise.

I put the book back in the drawer. I knew I had to get out of there fast.

"I gotta' go."

I ran out of his bedroom and down the steps. I slammed the backdoor, jumped on my bike and began to ride around the neighborhood.

Was my whole family sick? What is the big deal about naked bodies anyway? I bet his mother doesn't know about this!

When I arrived home, Daddy was waiting for me.

"Sit down" he demanded.

Oh no. He knew what happened.

I sat in Momma's favorite chair. I didn't want to talk to him. I didn't want to talk about what I had just read.

I hate you. You are a monster. You hurt everybody.

He stood tall over me. My insides were shaking. Was he going to yell at me? Was he going to cuss me out?

In that same calm voice he used some years ago when he talked to Momma about the picture he explained, " Roy told me that you read his book. None of it is true. I want you to stay away from down there, ya' hear me?"

"Yes."

"Okay," he ended and turned to go into his bedroom.

I went outside and got on my bike. I had to get away.

What does he mean that none of it is true? He lies so much. I hate him.

I went to the park and sat by a tree. I watched the mothers pushing their children on the swings.

My life doesn't make much sense. I sat with my elbows on my knees and my chin resting on my fists. I thought about some of the thing that went on in the past.....

****

"Clare, Clare! It's time for dinner."

"Wash your grubby little hands before you come to *my* dinner table," Momma played as she nodded her head towards the bathroom. She was standing by the kitchen counter mashing potatoes.

Daddy was already sitting at the table. As I turned on the water in the sink, I could hear them whispering. Daddy sounded upset.

I came in and sat down at the table. Daddy started in with one of his prayers.

"….and Father bless this food for the nourishment of our bodies for Christ's sake, Amen."

"Amen. Daddy, you sho' sound like a preacher."

"Ummph" was all I heard as he bit into a fried chicken back.

"Ya'll know that all of y'all women do it," he grumbled.

"Now Donny," Momma pleaded.

I could tell she was trying to get him to talk about something else. But he wasn't listening. He seemed determined to finish their conversation.

"Y'all sit on that front row of that church with your legs gapped open so that Pastor Rainer can look between your legs."

As they began to yell at each other, I imagined Momma and the other women on the front row with their legs opened.

How could Pastor Rainer see anything? Momma wore stockings and a girdle.

I took a few quick bites of food. My stomach started to hurt and I didn't feel like eating anymore. I slipped gently away from the table and went to my bedroom. They didn't seem to notice me leaving. My hands started to shake and I wanted to throw up. I was scared. This didn't sound good at all. I grabbed one of my teddy bears and sat on the floor by my bed. It wasn't long before I heard that rustling sound. I knew that Daddy was pushing Momma around. I stood by my bedroom door and waited for the sound to stop before I went into the kitchen.

Daddy was sitting at the table and Momma was crying as she stood against the wall with a glass in her hand. It was raised above her head and her hand was shaking.

I stood motionless at the kitchen door. My mind raced quickly. *Should I run across the street to Jamie's house and get help? He would probably kill her if she hit him. What would happen to me? Why did I have to live in a house like this?*

" I'll hit you with this glass," she threatened.

Sweat began to form at the top of my brow. I could feel my legs becoming weak and my feet felt like they weighed 100 pounds.

He continued to chew his food. He never looked up at her.

" I dare you." His voice sounded like a dog growling. "Go ahead, I dare you to hit me with that glass." With that he continued to eat.

I looked at Momma as she lowered the glass by her side. She looked hopeless. My hands started to sweat and my eyes began to burn with anger.

Hit him! Hit him across his bald head and maybe he'll leave you alone!

Suddenly Aunt Rachel knocked at the back door. She walked in as if she already knew what was going on.

" Clare," she stated in a very stern voice, "get your things, you're spending the night with me."

I didn't want to go home with her but I wanted to leave. I had heard and seen more than I wanted to.

****

I awoke out of this thought with a little boy yelling in my direction.

"Hey, throw the ball! Throw the ball!"

He was standing not too far from where I was sitting. His legs were covered with dirt and one of his shoe laces were untied. I threw the ball gently towards him.

"Here ya' go."

I got on my bike and started that long ride back home.

To Tell The Truth

Years have passed and my life has basically been the same, catching things and noticing things I really didn't want to know.

I used reading as a means of escape. It started with Dr. Seuss and Bible stories, then on to Donald Goines and Jive Magazine.

When I turned sixteen, Daddy bought me a car and told me it was time to get a job. I applied for a work permit at the high school I attended. Momma encouraged me to put in an application at the hospital where she was working. I was interviewed and offered a position as a part time school worker for the dietary department. The pay was really good. I made more than minimum wage and sometimes, if they were short of help, I worked a full eight hour shift on the weekends. Momma and I visited one another whenever we had a chance.

One afternoon, I came home to change clothes and prepare for work. I walked in the house and their were two neighborhood girls sitting at our kitchen table with my Father. Sherry and Susan were both fourteen and they had bad reputations for being girls who had sex.

I looked at Daddy with disgust on my face. I spoke to him, but made it a point not to speak to the girls. I took long strides to make it out of the kitchen and went straight to my bedroom. The door moved slowly across the dark blue carpet as I tried to slam it shut. It made a much softer noise than what I intended.

That dog is getting old, but he still likes to hunt. He doesn't know what else to do with his money. I know that's why they are here. He is giving them money for favors. He doesn't care who he takes advantage of. He knows these girls come from families that don't have much. This whole thing is making me sick. I hate dirty old men and my Father is one!

As quick as I could, I grabbed my uniform out of the closet and put it on. I slipped my white shoes on and without tying the laces, I left the house without a word.

When I arrived at work, Momma was waiting for me by the locker room as she sometimes would. The tears started uncontrollably rolling down my cheeks. Immediately her face showed concerned and she took steps to move closer to me.

"What's the matter Clare?"

I was trembling. I felt like the words were choking in my throat. My eyes burned with anguish and I felt the anger grow within my heart. I looked to my mother desperately for hope, for help. I just couldn't take it anymore. All of my life there had been one incident after another. A picture here, a naked person there, pornography books not put away, a lie here, a fight there. Something, *something* was always going on. I felt as if my emotions were tumbling down a long hill. I wanted to scream and just collapse to the floor. All of my energy was draining. I was tired of keeping all of the secrets.

I looked into her eyes and confided " I think Daddy is messing with Sherry and Susan and with your sisters too."

There. I had said it. Out loud. I had finally said to her what I had been holding since I was five years old. I stood there for what seemed like an eternity waiting for her to say something. In my mind, I was envisioning us going home, telling him we knew everything and pack our clothes to leave. I thought I was ready for whatever she said we needed to do until she spoke.

She stood there frozen. Her eyes were blank as if she was remembering another time. Her voice was quiet and as small as she seemed at that moment.
She sighed, "I know."

I wanted to scream at her. *Is that it! Is that all! You know!?!* But instead I looked at my mother. I really looked at her. I put my arms around her and hugged her. What I saw on her face was something that I despised. What I saw was.....defeat.

That evening I fumbled my way through work. The tears would not stop running down my checks. I went to the bathroom as often as I could to keep my face washed.

I was working in the dish room when a couple of my coworkers came to me. It was Cheryl and Olivia.

Cheryl was there, I knew to get all the information that she could to spread it around the department. Olivia had a look of genuine concern on her face.

"Are you okay?" Olivia asked almost in a whisper.

"Yeah," I said sarcastically. "I'm okay. My Father is just a dirty old man."

They both looked at me with surprise. Cheryl's eyes lit up. Her lips appeared to smack as if she had just eaten a sweet tart. Not knowing what to say to me, they walked away and began to whisper to each other. Cheryl kept looking back over her shoulder.

I continued to work and it wasn't long before my supervisor was there. Her name was Nadine. She was a very strict manager. She seemed to have eyes in the back of her head.

Without much concern she asked, "Do you need to go home?"

"Naw, I'll finish my shift."

"Well then, get those dishes off the rack and bring them out to the kitchen, the line needs them."

I guess she was trying to be nice, in a mean sort of way.

After work I didn't go straight home. I rode around for awhile trying to straighten the thoughts out in my head.

First thought. *Okay, I hate my father. He is a liar, a child abuser, a wife beater and a perverted sex maniac.*

Second thought. *I hate my mother. She is defenseless. She can't or won't stand on her own two feet and make a decision for herself or for me.*

Third thought. *Okay now, what about me? What about me? What am I gonna do? How could I continue to live like this? My options are limited, so I know that I'm gonna t have to go home. I can continue to work at the hospital and by the time I graduate, I'll get a full time position and move out.*

That's it. I'll get my own place and then I won't have to deal with this anymore. No matter what happens now, it's all just a matter of time for me and this will all be over.

With a plan in place, I went home.

****

A few months had passed and nothing at home had changed.

I arrived home from work one evening and I saw my mother's car at home. It surprised me because she was just at work earlier that afternoon. I walked into the house and immediately I knew something had happened. The television was not on. The radio was not on her favorite station. The quiet in the air was thick. Momma was sitting at the kitchen table. When I came in, her eyes met mine. They were swollen and red. From the kitchen I could see my parents bedroom. I could see Daddy lying on the bed with his legs crossed, reading the newspaper.

"What happened?" I began.

Without a word, she grabbed a pen, a piece of paper and began to write. When she finished, she handed me the note and turned her head to look out of the back window.

I looked at her for a moment. I didn't want to read the note. I just wanted this madness to be over. I looked at the piece of paper and it read: I caught your father and Rachel in bed together. Without a word, I put the note on the table. That old familiar feeling of hate began to rise in me again.

As I went to my bedroom, I spoke to my Father. I didn't want to but I knew I had better. I could only stay in the house for a few minutes. I quickly changed my clothes and got out of there. I felt like I was about to smother. I needed fresh air. I needed time to think.

As I drove around the city without a destination, I thought about my Father. He was some type of man. It seemed to me outside of devastating people's lives, he had his stuff together. Here he was, right after being caught, lying in the same bed reading his paper as though he were King Tut. He seemed untouchable, unstoppable. If anyone said anything to him that he didn't like, he would either cuss them out or beat them up.

I knew he was a madman, yet something inside of me admired the authority and control he had. I made up my mind, if this is how relationships are going to be then I was going to be the one in control. Not the victim. I hated the role of the victim.
****

After high school, I went away to college. It was so good to be away from home.

I really didn't want to go to college, but it was expected of me. I was only about an hour away so I was back on the weekends. I had a boyfriend who was a senior in high school.

I found out I was pregnant the first time at the age of 18. I had just started college. My father bought the groceries at our house and that included the kotex pads.

I was home from college one weekend and my father called me into the kitchen.

" I haven't bought you any Kotex pads lately," he stated. I felt he was probing for an explanation.

" I haven't needed any Kotex pads lately," I snipped kind of matter-of-factly.

I already knew I was pregnant. I hadn't taken a pregnancy test but I had experienced morning sickness. My periods came regularly and I already missed two.

I went into my bedroom and sat on my bed. I was pregnant by my high school sweetheart Roger. He was of no help to me at all.

My mother came into the bedroom and stood against the wall. She looked at me for a while without saying a word. There was sadness in her eyes.

She sounded like a mouse when she asked, "Do you think Roger's mother will allow him to marry you?"

Marry me? I didn't want to be married. Where were we going to live?

" Momma, I don't want to be married."

My father immediately took control of the situation. He looked in the newspaper and found an abortion clinic. He had made up his mind, I was going to have an abortion.

" I found a place to take you that is about an hour away. They will take care of this mess that you've gotten yourself into," he growled.

"How can you do this?" I protested.

"You are not going to embarrass me, being with that boy and you're not even married. Are you a fool? Don't you know that a man doesn't have to buy a cow if he has already tasted the milk?"

"You're a teacher in the church. You teach the Bible," I protested.

" That has nothing to do with this."

I looked to my mother for some support. She dropped her head and went into the kitchen to sit down. She was not going to help me.

I thought about running away to some of my family members in another city but I
decided against it because this was not their problem, it was mine.

The next morning my Father woke me up and told me to get

ready. His face looked like a piece of stone, hard with no concern. Fear and anger gripped me but I complied. I slept all the way to the clinc.

The building was a light brick color. We were the only ones in the waiting room. My father went to the window and gave the receptionist my name.

It wasn't long before a woman came to the door and called my name. I looked at my mother for a last hope of help. I could see in her eyes that she had been convinced this was the best thing.

When I got to the back, the woman told me to put on a gown and lay on the table. She gave me a shot and right away I became drowsy. She rolled me into another room.

"Open your legs." It was a man's voice. He sounded harsh without any sympathy.

I wanted to cry. I wanted to scream and run away but I couldn't move. I noticed a woman in the room, maybe she was the nurse. I looked to her with terror in my eyes, pleading for help.

She came close to my face and sneered, " You won't do *this* anymore will you? Will you?"

A tear managed to escape before I fell asleep. When I woke up my mother was there.

"Get your clothes on baby. It's time to go." She looked beat down but I could tell she was very concerned. She helped me get dress and we went to the car.

No one spoke a word. I went to sleep on the ride home.

When I got to my bedroom, I grabbed a pillow and clutched it to my stomach. I began rocking back and forth humming a song to my baby who was no longer there.

My father came and stood in the doorway. "What's wrong with you?" he asked.

My eyes glared back at him. I hated this man.

Just above a low grumble I said, "Nothing, nothing is wrong with me."

He looked at me for awhile with a puzzled look on his face. I was surprised too. That voice didn't sound like me.

****

I went back to college for a short period. I had made up my mind that I was going to be in control of my own life and nobody was going to tell me what to do anymore.

I hated my mother for not standing up for me. I hated my father for being such a hypocrite. I hated myself for not protecting my baby's life.

I left college, went back to work at the hospital and pick up another part-time job. When I had saved enough money, I bought some furniture and moved out of my parent's home.

Freedom at last! I didn't have to know or hear about anymore arguments. I could live my own life and finally be free of all of their garbage.

It didn't take long before my life started heading on its' own destructive course. I soon realized I was not free at all. I found myself having the same attitudes and desires as those I thought I left behind.

The Stage is Set

By the time I was pregnant the second time, I had married Roger. I didn't know that I was pregnant. I was smoking a lot of marijuana and I wasn't keeping up with my menstrual cycles.

I was working for a retail department store and I started experiencing a lot of stomach pain.

Jan was the manager that evening. She was an overachiever type and I really didn't want to approach her.

" Jan, something is wrong with me, I need to go home."

"Well can't you just sit down and rest for a few minutes? This is a busy time. We are having a big sale this weekend and I need help stocking."

"I don't think that I can stay," I said holding my stomach.

"Well….if you must go, go ahead then."

I drove myself home and Roger's car wasn't there. It struck me as strange because he had gotten off of work earlier that afternoon.

I was scared and I was hurting bad. I went to the living room floor and laid on the carpet by the heating register and fell asleep.

After awhile I heard the back door open.

"Come on in," Roger said.

Before I could say anything I heard another voice.

"Turn on the lights Roger." It was a woman. I stood up in the living room waiting for them to come all the way into the house.

"Yes, turn on the lights Roger so you can see me," I hissed.

I could see it was Blade. She was a friend of Roger's from high school.

"Oh, hi Clare, I didn't know you were home," Roger stammered.

" Blade, what are you doing here?" I questioned.

"Roger just wanted to show me the house but I guess I better leave now."

"Yeah, I guess you better." I went back into the living room and laid on the floor.

She left and Roger came into the living room.

"Where have you been Roger?"

"Blade was getting a new furnance put into her house and she didn't want to be there alone with a stranger, so I stayed until the work was done. What are you doing home?
Aren't you suppose to be at work?"

"Something's wrong with me Roger. I'm in a lot of pain."

" Do you want to go to the hospital?" he said trying to sound concerned.

I knew he was lying but at that moment I didn't care.

"Naw, I'll just go to bed and go into the doctor's office in the morning." I glared at him when I walked by. He kept his head bowed.

****

Roger got up early the next morning and went to work. I went to the doctor's office alone. He didn't ask if I wanted him to come along. At the doctor's office it was confirmed that I was pregnant but he sent me directly to another office to have an ultra sound.

I went into the office and they immediately took me in. Something was wrong and I knew it. The man who performed my ultra sound was very rude.

"Hello," I said as I entered the room.

" Get up on the table and lay on your back," the man grunted with just a glance in my direction.

As I was having the procedure done, I was looking at the screen but I couldn't tell what was going on.

"Is everything okay?"

"Not yet," he said with a smirk on his face. "You need to go back to your doctor's office right now."

When I arrived at the office my hands were shaking and tears were running down my face. I went into his office instead of an examination room.

"Clare, your baby is in your fallopian tube. It did not make it to your uterus. We call this an Eptopic pregnancy. If we don't remove this tube right away, you can die."

"May I please use your phone," I whimpered.

He left the room. I called my mother and told her to call Roger at work and for them to meet me at the hospital.

****

My father was sick at this time and he was going down hill mentally. My mother, my mother-in-law and Roger all showed up at the hospital. I told them what was going on. None of them said a word. They all sat there in silence. I knew this was a time I had to be strong, none of these people could do anything for me.

The surgeon came in to speak with me. " I want you to know you can still have babies with one tube left. My mother had seven children and she only had one tube. Everything is going to be just fine. I'm going to call in the anesthesiologist now to get you prepared."

I began to cry. I didn't care what happened with his mother. I had lost another baby. Another baby gone and still no babies in my arms.

When they came to roll me away to surgery, Roger finally approached the bed. I could see the terror in his eyes.

"Don't forget to wake up," he pleaded.

"Yeah," I said and they rolled me away.

****

When I arrived home, I cried a lot. It seemed every commerical on television was about baby bottles or diapers. It was a terrible loss but there was no one there to console me.

A few months later I found myself pregnant again. I was so happy. I was still smoking marijuana and by this time I was an everyday user. I knew I should stop, but I didn't.

One day I felt that same familiar pain in my stomach I had at the last pregnancy. I knew this baby was in my tube also. I immediately went to my bedroom, dropped to my knees and prayed.

I was raised in the church. I believed that God was real even though I wasn't living a good Christian life. I believed the story about Jesus and I was baptized at the age of seven. I believed Jesus was the Son of God.

"Lord, please don't let this baby be in my tubes. Please Jesus, I need your help. I want to have a baby Lord, please don't let this baby be in my tubes."

I laid on the floor and cried. Suddenly I stopped crying. There was a gentle peace that surrounded me.

A few mornings later I woke up to a wet bed. I was having a miscarriage. Blood was all over my clothes and my sheets. I went to the bathroom and called my doctor. He told me to come into his office.

I had a procedure called a D&C. The doctor told me I needed this procedure to scrape out my uterus so no particle of the baby was left.

"Clare, I am giving you a prescription for birth control pills. Please use them. You need to give your body a rest," he said empathetically.

I was devasted. *Baby number three.* I went into a deep depression.

****

My drug use intensified. I continued to smoke marijuana and I began to drink alcohol heavily. Anything to numb the pain of what my life had become. I didn't acquire a taste for beer so I drank things like, Malt Duck Wine, Seagram's Gin and Long Island Ice Tea.

I found myself getting drunk a lot but I justified it because I told myself I was at home and it was nobody's business.

Being in a world of drugs and alcohol, I was introduced to different types of people using all types of drugs. I used a stimulate called speed. It came in pill form and it gave me a sense of false energy. I could get a lot of things done but when the effect wore off, I was more depressed.

I also was introduced to a white powder called cocaine. I liked this drug because it gave me that "up" feeling again. There was a stigma attached to this particular drug. In the drug world I was "somebody" when I used this.

Roger seemed to know everybody who used drugs. He brought all sorts of people to the house. Nice people. They were friendly. There was a drug party at our house every weekend.

One day when I came home from work, I saw the light on in the basement. Roger was in the basement with my cousin Matthew. When I watched what they were doing, it looked so intimate, so inviting. I wanted to know what was going on.

Into the Pit

The basement was set up into three different rooms. There was a family room where we kept the televison. We also had a bathroom and a laundry room all in one. The kitchen was where I found them.

"Hey y'all, whatcha' doin?"

Roger had a small pipe in his mouth and Matthew was putting a flame to it.

"Hey Cuz," Matthew spoke quickly, his eyes fixed on the flame.

Roger took a long inhale. His eyes bulged as if he was getting ready to choke trying to hold in the smoke. When he finally blew it out, his forehead was beading with sweat.

"That was good man, that was really good," he mumbled as he swallowed beer out a bottle.

Matthew was putting the pipe up to his mouth next. There was something strange about the way they were acting. It looked cozy but it didn't feel right.

"I'll be back," I said. Neither one of them acknowledged me.

I went upstairs to my bedroom and found the stash of marijuana that I kept in my drawer. I came back downstairs and began to roll up a joint to smoke. After I took a couple of puffs I went into the kitchen to pass the joint around.

"Here you go, this is some good stuff."

Roger had the pipe again, this time he held his own flame.

"Naw Cuz, you go ahead," Matthew answered.

Roger exhaled the smoke he was holding. I handed the joint to him. He didn't say a word, he just shook his head no.

"Y'all don't want no weed?" I was confused. These were my smoking buddies.

"We'll be back." Roger stated.

Matthew was already wrapping the pipe up in a towel and putting it back on the counter.

"Where y'all goin' ?"

"To get some more crack." Roger sounded irritated as he was digging into his pockets counting his money.

"Some more what?"

"Crack Cuz, it's called crack. Don't mess with this stuff 'til we get back," Matthew instructed.

"Don't worry, I'll be here smoking all this weed by myself."

They left in a hurry without saying good-bye.

I put some clothes in the washing machine and warmed up grease on the stove to fry chicken. It was a beautiful day. I had started to get over my feeling of losing my last baby. Life without kids wasn't so bad after all.

I was turning the chicken over when they returned. "Hey, that didn't take long," I said as they came in the door.

They went straight downstairs.

I followed along behind them watching as I saw them putting what looked like a little white rock into the hole of the pipe. The only time they spoke was when Matthew was giving Roger instructions on what to do.

"Hey, do you think I can try it?" I whined feeling left out.

Roger stared at me with a strange look. In his eyes I thought I saw fear. "Naw, you can't try it."

"What do you mean I *can't* try it? You are in my basement smoking dope and I can't have any?"

"I don't want you doin' it. Just go upstairs and smoke your weed and be happy."

" I can't believe that y'all are this greedy. Keep your dope." I stomped up the stairs and rolled up another joint. *Who does he think he is? I have my own dope, I don't need them.*

I heard them later going out of the door again. Coming and going. Coming and going. This lasted until I fell asleep. I didn't understand but I knew something had come into my home which wasn't good.

****

I was a demanding person. What I want, I got. It didn't take long for me to wear Roger down. I think his guilt helped a lot too.

Crack cocaine was a high I never experienced before. A piece of it was called a "rock." It looked like a small white rock one could find outside in a driveway. I began to hear about the effects of people using this drug. They stopped having contact with people who weren't using. They took their possessions to the pawnshop and sold them for money to buy dope. They lost their children to child protective services. They lost their homes and their cars. There was a special program on television which talked about crack cocaine becoming an epidemic in the United States. Family members, old schoolmates, people in my neighborhood, it seemed as if everybody I knew was smoking crack. I fooled myself into believing what I saw and heard about other people was not going to happen to me. This drug made me not want to do anything else but get high.

It wasn't like that at first though. I could smoke a little piece, still wash clothes and hang them on the line. I could smoke a little piece and still go to the grocery store. But one day it bit me like a venomous snake. The posion was in my body and I couldn't seem to get it out. I found myself craving it all the time.

Crack became the answer to all of my problems. Any excuse to use crack would do. The water bill is due. I needed a rock. The tire on my car was flat. I needed a rock. Roger had upset me. I needed a rock. It's pay day. Time to celebrate. I needed a rock. I'm broke, I spent all of my money on drugs and I didn't pay any of my bills. I needed a rock.

****

At this time, my father lay dying in the hospital. I didn't visit him often because my total world was surrounded by drug use. I felt bad about not going to see him like I knew I should. So to cover that bad feeling, I got high.

My father passed away after a long term stay in the nursing home and the hospital in January of 1989. My drug use intensified. My job had given me extra days off with grievance pay. All I did, day and night was smoke crack. Roger at the time was my supplier. I stayed in the house and waited on the drugs to come.

After the funeral, I went back to work but I never stopped getting high. Many times I stayed up all night, took a shower right before work and go in feeling the lingering effects from smoking dope and lack of sleep.

One day I came to myself. My father was dead and no matter how much I smoked drugs he was never coming back. The seasons had changed and it was late spring. I sat on the front porch of my home. My senses awoke and I was amazed that the grass had turned green and the children were riding their bikes and playing outside. I realized that I had been getting high and not living my life at all. It was time to stop. My clothes were falling off of me because I wasn't eating properly. My mind began to change and I knew there was a better way of life for me, but Roger did not want to stop. He did not stop. I didn't either. Everytime the drug came into my home, I used it. I hated him and I hated myself. I felt like we were in a hole in the ground and I was trying to get out but he kept pulling me back down. I knew in order to save my life I needed to get out of this relationship. I didn't have the strength to leave on my own and go back to my mother's home. The drugs were so much a part of my life I didn't know what to do.

I needed to clear my head so I took a walk to the neighborhood store. When I arrived there, I saw my old neighborhood girlfriend Jamie. She had put on a lot of weight. She had on jeans and her shirt was on the outside of her pants, pulled down over her stomach. She looked at me with a mixture of surprise and sympathy. It had been awhile since we saw each other.

"Clare?" she gasped with her head tilted.

"Hey, Jamie girl, how ya' doin?" I tried to sound cheerful even though I knew I looked like dirt.

"I'm doing fine girl, …how are you?"

"I'm okay. It was good seeing ya girl, let me finish my shoppin'," I said walking away from her down the aisle. I had to get away from her. The burning look in her eyes were telling me all I needed to know about myself. I looked bad. My clothes were not ironed and I hadn't done anything to myself to look appealing. I couldn't get away fast enough before I heard her voice calling me.

"Hey Clare."

I stopped and put on a smile before I turned around. "Yeah, what's up?"

"Do you remember Sam from school?"

"Sam Andrews, yeah I remember him."

" He's been asking about you."

I met Sam in elementary school. He was one of the boys I used to talk dirty with on the phone when I was in the 6th grade.

"Really, the last I heard about him, he was in Nevada going to college," I replied.

She couldn't tell that I wanted this conversation to be over because she kept right on talking. "Naw girl, he's back now working at Humphrey's, the adult foster care.

"Well the next time you see him, tell him I said hello." With that last comment, I turned and walked away.

On my way back home, I thought about Sam. He was a nice looking guy. We were friends in junior high and high school. Maybe this was what I needed. Someone who was interested in me. Someone who was not on drugs.

The next day when Roger went to work, I got the telephone number of Humphrey's out of the phone directory.

It wouldn't hurt if I called my old friend just to say hello, since he was asking about me.

I called the number and a young lady answered the phone. I could hear the television in the background.

"Hello, is Sam Andrews available?"

"Yes, could you hold please? Sam, the phone is for you," I heard the woman say as she put the phone down.

In just a few moments he was on the other end. "Hello." His voice sounded the same.

I felt a little nervous. "Hi Sam, I heard you've been asking about me, how are you?" I didn't want to let him know who I was right away. I wanted to play with him first.

"I'm fine, who is this?"

"Do you always ask about a lot of women? This is Clare."

"Hey Clare, who told you I asked about you?"

"I saw Jamie at the store and she mentioned it."

"So you looked me up at work and called me. That's a nice surprise. I'm busy right now though and I get off at 2:00 o' clock. Can you call me back at home later?"

"Sure," I said without giving it a second thought.

He gave me his home phone number and we hung up. I was excited. This was something that I had to look forward to other than using drugs. I wanted anything that would help me escape.

Later on I called Sam and found out he graduated from

college in Nevada. He was back home now living with his mother and working as well as filling in at the School Administration office. He asked me if I would come and see him sometime and I did. We started spending time together just talking and catching up.

Roger had missed so many days at work, in order to keep his job at General Motors he had to go into a drug treatment center for 30 days.

I was glad Roger was gone. It was a relief. I didn't smoke crack the whole time he was away but I still smoked weed. I no longer had to sneak around to see Sam, so our time together increased. I invited him over one night to visit and that night him and I became lovers.

When Roger got home from the treatment center I really hoped things would be better but they got worse. As soon as he got home, he bought some crack cocaine and my life of drug use started again.

In this drug circle we heard of many other people who we knew were on crack. Roger told me about a guy named James who went to high school with us that was in the treatment center also. I remembered James being a good friend of Sam's in high school. They played on the basketball team together. I thought to myself that the city we lived in was really a small place. What were the chances of Roger being in the same treatment center at the same time with one of the friends of the guy I was now seeing.

My husband had no idea that I was in an adulterous relationship, he kept right on talking. "Yeah," he said as smoke was coming out of his mouth, he looked like a chimney, "James told me that he used to smoke crack with Sam Andrews too. Do you remember Sam? I never thought he would be smoking this stuff. You never know who's doin' what. I'm not surprised. Everybody is doin' it. The treatment center was packed and they said crack was now becoming an epidemic. Are you ready for your hit?"

I felt like the wind had been knocked out of me. I'd been living a fantasy thinking Sam was my escape out of the drug world. I just didn't want to believe it.

Roger noticed the strange look on my face and asked me what was wrong.

"I'm just surprised so many people are smoking this stuff."

There was a knock at the door and some of Roger's buddies came in ready to celebrate his return.

With Roger being distracted, I went upstairs to call Sam. I was going to ask him face to face.

Another Life

I picked Sam up and we went to a nearby park to talk.

"By the look on your face, I can tell that something has happened, what's wrong?" he asked as he reached for my hand.

I moved my hand before he could touch it. I choked back the tears. My mouth did not want to say the words but they slowly came out, "Are you smoking crack?"

He hesitated a minute, turned his head toward the window and deeply sighed, "Yes." He looked back at me, "How did you find out?"

I told him about the conversation Roger and I had earlier. He saw the disappointment on my face.

"Will you still see me?" he asked.

"I don't know," the tears began to pour down my face. I drove him back to his house and went back home. I got high for many days.

****

Things at my home were getting worse. Roger began to deal with teenagers who were selling dope. He began to "rent" our cars to them for drugs. Sometimes we would get the cars back right away, sometimes it took days.

I kept in touch with Sam from time to time. We still managed to spend time together but we didn't smoke crack. I think it was my time away from drugs as well as his.

Finally in August of 1989 I was fed up with Roger and this lifestyle. He had no intention of getting better and my life was going down hill fast. I had managed to keep my job as a receptionist at a nursing care facility and through that job I was offered another position at a facility which sent health care aides to different homes. I carried a pager and staffed these facilities throughout the weekend. I asked Sam's mother could I rent out a room at her house. While Roger was at work, I packed up a few things and I left leaving all of the furniture and took a few things to my mother's home for storage. Roger never asked me to come back. He allowed a local street whore to move in with him. My marriage was over.

****

Sam and I took walks together and talked. Little did we know lurking behind the corner was a ugly monster who would appear in our relatonship also.

One day while watching Jeopardy, a beautiful white Cadillac pulled into the driveway. The man was someone that Sam knew. He stood tall in his jeans and tee shirt. He was dark complexed, with average features.

When he walked in the house his voice was cheerful and loud. "Anyone here want some narcotics?"

Sam introduced us. His name was Darnell. He had a friendly

disposition.

"Come on man," he said as he headed for the basement. Apparently he had been there before.

It had been awhile since I had smoked crack but my stomach began to feel that familiar turn whenever the drug was around. Sam looked at me and followed Darnell downstairs. I followed Sam, knowing deep inside me this was the beginning of the end for our relationship.

Here I am in a different house with a different person doing the same thing I used to do.

By this time, I was so depressed about my marriage and everything that I had lost. Smoking crack with Sam made me lose all my self-respect and any respect I had for him. I never wanted him to see me use crack.

The world I knew changed even more when I found out Sam's mother, Rayscene smoked crack also.

One day I came home early from work. Sam still had a few more hours left before his shift was over. When I walked into the house there were three guys I didn't know sitting on the couch watching television.

"Hey, who are you?" I asked the first guy who glanced my way. He must have been the leader because the others never stop watching television.

"My name is Jay. Who are you?"

"I'm Clare, did Rayscene let you in?"

"Yeah, we gonna be staying here awhile."

I went to my bedroom. I noticed that Rayscene's door was closed.

"Rayscene," I called as I knocked then opened her door.

She was smoking dope with her friend named Kelly. "Here," she said as she passed me a large portion of dope.

"Who are those guys in the living room?" I asked as I held the dope in my hand.

"They are dealers from Mayville. They will be staying here for awhile. They paid me to rent out the house to them." She put another piece of dope in her pipe, while Kelly was looking on the floor as if she had dropped some.

I went to my room and called Sam to let him know what was going on. I smoked some of the dope while waiting on him to come home. This was a world that I had never known. Sam did not approve at all but we both felt like we didn't have anywhere else to go. We would get up and go to work and the dealers were there. When we got home from work they were there. There were people that we didn't know coming to the house buying, selling and using dope. There were women coming in selling their bodies. I had a little room in the back that seemed to be getting smaller all of the time.

One day I came home from work and there was a police car in

the driveway. I went in to see what was going on. There had been a drug bust and they had the guys in custody.

When I walked in one of the police officers quickly approached me. "Who are you?"

"My name is Clare, I am renting a room in the back."

"Do you have any identification?" This policeman was serious. The lines in his face were drawn tight. In his eyes, I could not spot one twinkle. I gave him my driver's license. "You sure have lost a lot of weight," as he studied my picture. I felt as if he was trying to remember me from somewhere but I knew that he didn't. He gave me my identification. I went to my bedroom. When I came back out, everyone was gone except me. Sam was at work. Only God knew where Rayscene was.

Things went on as before the raid. Rayscene found some more people to come in and sell dope. Not having food in the house became a way of life. We began to get high off of all the money that we could find. I met some of Rayscene's friends who taught me how to "boost." We went to different department stores and stole clothes, purses, jewelry, whatever we could and then sold the merchandise to people for drug money.

About three months later, I came home from work and their was several police cars at the house and the neighbors were outside. Sam saw me come up, he was across the street and called me over. There had been another raid but this one was not as clean. When everybody left, Sam and I decided to go home. The house was a disaster. There was a whole in the living room ceiling. We found out later that one of the guys ran upstairs to hide in the attic and the floor gave in. The water pipes in the basement were busted. Everything was a mess. Our dresser drawers had been opened and clothes were everywhere. Our mattresses were turned off of our beds too.

"Clare, come here!"

I ran to the living room.

"Look," he said with a mixture of fear and disbelief. In his hand was three pieces of crack cocaine.

As we began to look around we saw pieces of crack all over the house. I stayed with him a little while but I went across the street. I was afraid the police would come back. Sam stayed and when I saw him again, he was loaded with crack cocaine. I had never seen so many rocks before. We got high in that neighbors' house all weekend. Everytime I thought the dope was gone, Sam would pull out another piece. I knew that I no longer could live in that house, they destroyed it for that purpose. Everyone was going to have to move.

I got up enough courage to ask my mother could I come back home.

****

Going back home proved to be a difficult thing to do. My

mother did not trust me and she had every right not to. I was in and out all of the time. I found out that Roger and his mother were staying at a neighbor's house. I don't know where I got the nerve but I asked my mother could Roger live with us. We stayed with her for three months. We were heavy drug users. We only used her house to eat and sleep. Roger and I managed to keep

our jobs. My mother was my transportation back and forth to work.

One day we left a little early and stopped at Burger King. I knew that it had been a while since my last period so I had her stop by the store and I secretly picked up a pregnancy test. When we arrived at the resturant, I went into the bathroom to see what the results were. It took only a few minutes for me to see the positive mark on the test. I was pregnant again!

I went back to the table.

"Everything okay?" My mother's voice sounded as if she already knew.

"Yeah, everything is fine." I ate my breakfast without tasting it. I felt as though I was in a daze.

****

Pregnant. Pregnant. I'm having a baby? Here I am in an adulterous relationship and I'm pregnant. I've only been separated from Roger for five months. This is my fourth

pregnancy. Will I keep this one? Can my body even hold a baby?
I'm an addict. I can't take care of myself. I sure don't want the
responsibility of taking care of a baby. Sam is not someone I can
depend on. But...... there is a baby growing on the inside of me.
Can this baby be God's answer to all of my problems?

That day at work was a busy one. We had two meetings, one
with the Director and then one right after with Karen, the office
manager.

"Business is dropping off. There is another Health Care
Agency that opened and some of our aides are now working for
them," Karen said.

I saw her lips moving but I wasn't paying attention. My mind
was imaging what Sam was going to say when I told him about
the baby. I wondered about Roger's reaction to this news. I did
not want to be at work that day but I managed to smile, answer
the phones and get through it. My mother picked me up at
5:00pm.

"Hey Momma, have you seen Sam?"

"Not today," she said. I could tell by the tone of her voice she
didn't care if she'd ever see him again.

When we arrived home I went upstairs and immediately began
to call some of his
friends. Finally late that night I got an answer.

"Hello."

"Hello David, this is Clare. Have you seen Sam today?"

David was a tall dark skinned man that Sam had met playing city baseball. We had gotten high with him on a few occasions.

"Yeah, he just left to go and buy some more dope. He'll be back."

I hung up the telephone without saying goodbye. I had eight dollars and some change in my purse. I called a taxicab to pick me up. It was 2:00am when the driver arrived.

"Clare, where are you going?" Momma asked. She woke up when the driver blew his horn.

"I'll be back Momma. I found Sam," I answered going out of the back door.

While on the way, my mind raced in several directions. I wanted to get high. I wasn't sure if I had enough money to pay the cab driver to take me to the other side of town. *I'll keep my eyes on the meter and when it gets close to what I have, I'll just tell him to let me out.*

I was afraid to tell Sam. Also I was angry with myself for not using protection.

When we made it to the house, I paid the fare with only twelve cents left.

David opened the door. "Clare?" He was surprised to see me. I hadn't told him I was coming. "Sam hasn't made it back yet, come on in."

He had his crack pipe in his hand. He rented an upstairs apartment house. His house was dark except in the kitchen. On the table there were cotton balls, pieces of charboy, a couple of cigarette lighters and Barcardy 151 Rum. I noticed David had his pipe turned toward the kitchen light looking for any speck of residue that might have been left from the dope.

I went in the living room to wait. I wasn't sure if Sam was coming back or not. Tears began to roll down my face. I laid on the couch clutching my stomach until I fell to sleep.
I was awakened by Sam's voice just before daybreak. He wasn't too happy to see me laying on his friend's couch. David had covered me up with his bathrobe and it didn't look good.

"What are you doing here?" His voice was full of disgust.

I didn't care because I was angry too. He had been gone all night, didn't call me once and was getting high without me. I sat up on the couch. I had brought the results from the pregnancy test with me. I didn't say a word. I threw the test results at him.

"What is this?" he asked with a frown.

"It's the result of a pregnancy test. I'm pregnant!"

"So." He threw it back at me.

I wasn't shocked. I wasn't mad. All I wanted was some dope. We stayed there and smoked crack until mid-afternoon. His friend drove us back to my mother's house.

After the dope wore off, I was depressed. I hadn't felt this low after using in a while.

I wrote on a mirror upstairs in lipstick: **I am pregnant by an irresponsible man. I do not want a baby by an irresponsible man.** I cried myself to sleep.

****

The idea of having a baby began to sink into my head. I told my mother and other friends and family. What a mess my life had turned out to be. I'm married but I'm pregnant by another man and I'm addicted to crack.

It was mid- February of 1990. I had terrible morning sickness. I went to the doctor and he gave me pre-nantal vitamins. To me they looked like pills for a horse. I never took any of them.

By March I decided it was time to move out of my mother's home and find a place of my own. It was a clean two -story house with a two bedroom apartment upstairs. I tried to stop getting high on my own and just watch Sam and his friends but that didn't work. The drug dealers were standing right out on the street corner.

In May, I enrolled myself in an out-patient drug treatment program. It was a thirty day program and I was able to stay clean during that time. I was determined. There were reports on the news almost nightly about baby's being born addicted to crack cocaine. I didn't want that for my baby.

During the time I stayed clean, I began to attend the church I grew up in. I could feel that old time religion welling up inside of me again. I sang spiritual songs and hymns to my unborn child. It was difficult living with someone who smoked crack. I could see and smell the dope. After awhile, I couldn't take it any longer, I began to use drugs again. I told myself that pregnant women smoked cigarettes and their babies turned out okay. But every time I took a hit of crack, I imagined my baby choking on the smoke. I knew that it wasn't good but I could not stop. I was tormented.

In June, I felt the baby move in my stomach for the first time. It felt like a flutter of a butterfly. At first I was scared and then I was excited. *I've got to stop smoking crack! There is a life growing on the inside of me.*

My mother's home was a fifteen minute walk from my house, so I began to visit her. I substituted crack for fruit with salt. That changed in the middle of July.

More Than One Miracle

It was a really nice summer day. I decided to walk to the store and get a pop. I felt really good about myself. It was amazing how clear my mind was when I didn't smoke crack. As I was turning the corner I could smell barbecue cooking on someone's grill. The clouds were hanging in the sky like huge cotton balls. Children were riding their bikes. Some boys from the neighborhood were playing street ball.

I was feeling okay until I got to the store. This was the street corner that drugs were sold on. As I approached the store, I saw a pregnant woman buying crack. I passed by this corner for the last two weeks and it never bothered me, but this day was different. As I walked closer my stomach began to churn with the urge of smoking a piece of dope. I went over to where the transaction was taking place.

"Hey, what's up girl, whatcha' want today? I got dimes and twenties." The young dope dealer showed me the rocks in his hands.

I should walk away. I should just go home. Just leave. My mouth began to water and I said, "Give me a dime."

"Where are you goin?" the young pregnant lady asked me while examining her drugs.

"I'm goin' home. You wanna come?" I turned and walked

away. She was by my side. We didn't say a word to each other on the way back to my house. I felt a mixture of excitement and defeat. I knew that this wasn't right but yet something stronger on the inside of me had taken over again.

We got to my house and I pulled out Sam's straight shooter. This was a small version of a crack pipe that he preferred. This young lady appeared to be in her 7th or 8th month. She was big. After hitting my first piece of dope the overwhelming feeling of guilt surrounded me.

"We shouldn't be doin' this," I said.

"Doin' what?" she asked as if she didn't have a clue what I was talking about.

"Smokin' dope. What about our babies?"

"You pregnant?" She looked at me in disbelief.

I had not begun to show much at all. I wore medium sized clothes instead of maternity clothing.

"Yeah," I said, " a little over 5 months."

She didn't answer. We smoked one rock and then began to smoke the other one. On the first hit of the other rock, my baby suddenly jumped on the inside of me.

"That's it, I *can't* do this mess anymore. I'm hurting my baby." I sat down and watched her smoke the rest of the dope. When the drugs were gone, she began to take off her blue jean smock.

"What are you doin'?" I scolded.

She was looking down on the floor as if she had dropped some of the dope. She never looked at me. "I bought this from the Kmart store. We can take it back and get some money." She kept licking her lips and looking around frantically.

"You gotta' go," I insisted as I began to wrap the straight shooter back into a towel.

She left and I never saw her again.

Six days later I started to experience terrible pain. I thought it was heartburn. I hurt throughout my whole body all day. I couldn't sleep. I couldn't eat. It hurt to lay down and to sit up. My mind kept telling me that something was wrong but I knew that it was too early to have my baby.

Sam was going on a trip with his job for the weekend. They were going to Pictured Rocks in the Upper Peninsula of Michigan. He suggested that I spend time with my mother so that I wouldn't be home alone. Late that evening, I arrived at my mother's still in pain.

"What's wrong honey?" she asked.

"Momma, I just don't feel right. I hurt all over,especially in my chest."

"Do you want to go to the hospital?"

"Naw, I'll just wait to see the doctor in the morning." I was up all night.

When we got to the doctor I was taken in right away because I was pregnant. As soon as I told him my symptoms, he examined me and told my mother to get me to the hospital right away. I was diagnosed with severe Pre-Eclampsia and HELP syndrome. The doctor said my blood pressure was too high and they had to get the baby out of me in order to save my life. I had to have an emergency Cesarean section and I was told not to expect my baby to live. They quickly began to prepare me for surgery. One of the nurses came in to do an ultra sound. I saw a clear picture of my baby for the first time on the monitor. They told me that it was a girl and she was sucking her thumb. I called Sam's mother so that his family would know what was going on.

My baby was going to die. I was going to have to prepare a funeral for her. This is all of my fault. I don't deserve to be a mother. Another baby..... dead! Tears fell from my eyes as they rolled me into surgery. The surgical room was cold. There were a lot of people moving around in gowns and masks. The anesthesiologist came close to my face.

"I'm going to give you something to put you to sleep."

I nodded my head.

******

When I opened my eyes, I could not speak. My throat hurt as if I was beginning to catch a cold. My hands were tied down to the side of the bed.

A nurse came immediately into the room. "You're awake," she said. Her voice was soft and kind. She continued as she untied my arms, " You were fighting us, so we had to tie you up. You have a baby girl. Would you like to see her?"

I was talking but I didn't know if she could understand me, so I nodded my head.

She brought in a picture. What I saw was something that looked like a baby with a hat on in an incubator.

"What do you think?" she asked with a wide smile on her face.

I gave her a sign with my hand that I thought she was okay. I drifted back to sleep.

When I woke again, my mother was sitting in a chair next to my bed. "I thought you were going to die." She slumped down in the chair. She looked exhausted.

The doctor came in and took the tube out of my throat. I gagged as it came out.

No wonder I thought I was catching a cold, something was stuck down in my throat.

The nurse came in and asked me what was my daughter's name.

"Clarise," I whispered.

Sam's mother came in. "They had to get a ranger to find Sam, he is on his way home now." I went back to sleep.

I found out after my surgery that I began to have severe bleeding. That was from the HELP syndrome which leads to uncontrollable hemorrhaging. That's why I was in Intensive Care. My close relatives gathered around to encourage me never to have anymore children. I could tell they had been scared too.

When the bleeding slowed and I grew stronger one of the nurses put me in a wheelchair and took me to see my baby. As she rolled me passed the other incubators, I looked at the babies. Some had wires connected to them, some didn't. It felt like a cold place to keep a newborn baby.

The severity of Clarise's condition began to dawn on me as I was rolled up to where she slept. She was laying there and I could not touch her. She had a respitory tube in her throat. Needles and wires were hooked up all over her tiny body. She weighed one pound and two ounces at birth. She was so small they laid her on top of a diaper.

The doctor came to speak to me. "She is very sick. We are doing all that we can but we are not hopeful that she will make it. We just have to wait and see."

The nurse wheeled me back to my room. I don't know what hurt more, the pain in my body from the surgery or my heart after seeing my child.

****

The day came when I was released to go home, but Clarise

had to stay. I wasn't home long before the drug cycle started again. The drug dealers were still on the corner by the store. Nothing had changed, including me.

There were calls coming from the hospital saying that Clarise was not doing well. I didn't visit her everyday but my mother did.

My mother would call and she was angry. "Clare, have you even been to the hospital today to see yo' baby?"

"Naw Ma, I'm going later." I would say that so she would leave me alone.

I was free now to use drugs and not have to be concerned about being pregnant.

I haven't had this kind of freedom in months. There's nothing I can do for her anyway. I'm not a doctor or a nurse. They won't even let me touch her.

One day when I answered the phone the nurse was frank. "Hello, Clare, you need to come to the hospital right away."

"What's wrong?" I wanted to know details.

The nurse explained that my questions would be answered when I got there.

When I arrived the doctor told me that her condition was worse. She wasn't thriving as they had hoped and he didn't expect her to make it another day.

I stared at my baby in that incubator. It looked like every

breath added more stress to her small frame. From somewhere deep within me, I could hear an old hymn that I learned as a child, *Take you burdens to the Lord and leave them there.* I began to hum the melody of the song as tears rolled down my cheeks. I knew inside of me that my baby was not going to die. I believed that there was a God, whether I was living like it or not, God was *still* God.

I went home that afternoon and sat on my front porch with a hymnbook and sung all the hymns that I knew.

I began to pray. "God, I know that my life is messed up. There is no doubt about that but my baby is innocent of all that I have done. She does not deserve to die because of the lifestyle that I lived while she was inside of me. Please God, save my baby."

The next day I went to the hospital. The doctor came in to see me. "Clare, you have a strong little girl. I can tell because she is fighting."

The next day came and her condition went from critical to stable again. With that type of security in mind, I started getting high again.

In September I was able to hold her in my arms for the first time. My mother took me to the hospital. Only the parents could go into the nursery. She stood outside of the window. The nurse took a picture and gave it to me. She was so small. There was still something wrong. I felt like we didn't know each other. I didn't have any feelings for my baby. No love. No hate. Nothing. I said and did all the right things. I rocked her, kissed her and called her cute and funny names. But that feeling that a mother should have for her daughter was missing. I gave her back to the nurse. It was time to get high.

The summer left and the fall came. Clarise was still in the hospital gaining weight and coming along well. I was getting high like never before. I would occasionally stop by and visit her.

She was allowed to come home in November, weighing four pounds and eight ounces. My family and Sam's family came over to celebrate her arrival.

Clarise had been home about a month when I realized that I was pregnant again. I made an appointment to see my doctor. With all of my drug use, I weighed 99 pounds.

"Hello Clare." I felt like he was looking through me.

"Hello Dr. Chadwick. I want this pregnancy terminated." I could see what I interpreted as agreement in his eyes.

"Looking at your history and in light of what happened at the birth of your daughter, I would suggest that you have a procedure which will prevent anymore pregnancies. I could do them both at the same time."

"That's fine. When can I get in."

"I'll have my office call you when we get it scheduled.

The procedure was done in the hospital as an outpatient. My mother kept Clarise. I told her I had a follow -up appointment.

As soon as I got back home, I told Sam to go and get me some dope. I was in so much emotional pain that I needed to escape. Somewhere in my mind, I told myself when Clarise came home, I was going to stop getting high. That soon disappeared when the first opportunity presented itself.

It was different getting high with a baby in the house. Sometimes there was so much smoke that I had to put her in another room. I never really enjoyed my high with her being there. She may need changing or feeding or something and I secretly resented her for that. I would try and time my highs around her sleeping times. I found out the best time to get high was at night. The problem with that was after I had been up all night I wanted to sleep during the day but I couldn't.

With her being a premature baby, a nurse was assigned to come over once a week for three months. I hated the thought of someone coming to the house because I feared being caught, and them taking her away. Every time she was scheduled to come, I tried to make sure that I wasn't getting high. I would clean up the house and have Clarise in a nice outfit. The visits usually went the same.

"You are doing a really good job. The baby's weight is picking up and she looks healthy. Do you have any questions for me Clare?" She was a nice lady. Very professional.

Yes, I have a question. When are you going to leave? "No. I really appreciate you coming out and checking on her. It helps me to know that I am doing the right thing."

I tried to function as best I could. I went to church. I went to the grocery store and I took Clarise to all of her doctor's appointments. But I couldn't keep it up, the drug, as usual was taking it's rightful place.....first.

It turned into a vicious cycle. I was unable to keep diapers for her. I would take them back to the store and get money for drugs. Then I would go to the store and steal an expensive purse and take it back so that I could buy diapers again. I was on the government welfare system. I would receive food stamps every month. Sometimes on food stamp day I was able to make it to the grocery store. Most of the time I could only make it to the corner store where I traded my stamps for money to buy drugs. When the drugs were gone, I would go to the grocery store with a big purse and steal food. We were constantly moving from one house to the next because I used the rent money to buy drugs. There were times we lived without running water. I used the neighbors outside hose to fill a bucket to cook food, wash dishes and flush the toilet.

The day Clarise took her first steps there were people sitting in my living room getting high. I would smoke a piece of crack, stand her up against a wall and call her to myself. I could not celebrate it as other mother's could because of the effects of the drugs in my life.

When we celebrated her second birthday, I returned all of her gifts for the money.

****

The summer had gone and we were in the winter months. The house was dreary. No life. I was depressed. Sam and I had ended our relationship. The Christmas tree leaned against the wall with no bulbs and no presents. I wanted some dope. Everything I tried turned up with no luck. No one would give me any money. I went to the different stores to steal but I had an uncomfortable feeling so I left. I decided to do something that I had never done before. I was going to the drug house and offer the dealer sex for drugs. With my baby in my arms, I knocked on the door. No one answered. I beat on the door. No one came. I went back to my car, put Clarise in her seat and cried uncontrollably. I prided myself on being able to steal and manipulate for drugs. Now, in my mind I had sunk to an all time low. I managed to pull myself together and drive home. I couldn't stand to live like this anymore. *You should just kill yourself. You are not worth anything to your baby or anyone else. You didn't even buy anything for your daughter for Christmas. Do her and everyone else a favor, end your miserable life. End it!!* This was not the first time I had thought of killing myself but the thoughts were stronger than ever before. I sat on the floor with Clarise in my arms. The tears felt like hot lava on my cheeks. My daughter was so beautiful.

Did I really want to leave her in this world without me? No! No, I didn't want to leave her. I didn't want to die.

I realized that I could no longer blame my parents, Roger or Sam.

"Do you want Momma to stop gettin' high?" I cried staring into Clarise's eyes.

That day in December of 1992, by the grace of God, I made a decision that smoking crack was no longer going to be a part of my life.

A New Direction

Early the next morning I arrived at my mother's house. She was preparing for a program which was held by an organization she was in.

"Hi Grannay," Clarise said rushing to my mother.

"How's granny's baby?" I could tell my mother wasn't quite as happy to see me. We never discussed it but I knew that she was fed up with my behavior.

"Momma, I have made a decision," I began slowly.

"Oh?" she said as she shuffled through the papers on the table.

"Yeah," I continued. "Will you please keep Clarise while I go to a drug treatment center."

"I knew that was what you were gonna say," she replied. Instead of being proud of me, I felt my mother was ashamed.

After I arrived, I called Sam to let him know I had checked myself in.

"Hi Sam. I wanna let you know that Clarise is with Momma and I'm in the treatment center."

"Why would you even go to a place like that? Couldn't you just stop by yourself?" he moaned. I heard what I thought was disgust in his voice.

Neither Sam or my mother thought it was a good idea. I didn't understand their feelings but I knew I had to do this for myself.

During the time in the facility the counselor tried to convince me I needed to go away to another center for ninety days. I knew I couldn't because it was not my mother's responsibility to care for Clarise, it was mine. I left the treatment center after three days. My mother loaned me the money and she took me from house to house to pay off my drug debts.

I began to go to Cocaine Anonymous meetings but I was very lonely. All of the people I got high with, I had to leave alone. I had no other people to talk to and I didn't know these people at all. On February 4th the loneliness got to me and I smoked crack with my neighbor. I went and confessed it the next day at a meeting and they told me to "keep coming back." February 5th 1993 was the first day I counted as a "clean" day.

I kept going to meetings. I moved out of the neighborhood into a house that was one street block away from my mother. I applied for a job and within 30 days of being drug free and I was hired as a waitress.

The people I met at the meetings were very good at helping me to stay sober. But even though I was not using drugs there was still a empty space in my life that needed to be filled. I felt a lot better about myself but that hole in my life lead me to a new addiction.....sex.

I had sex with everyone that I thought I wanted to. Some times I had sex when I didn't want to but it was better than being alone. I began to get a terrible reputation of being a whore.

It was November of 1994 that I grew tired once again, of my way of life. I went back to the church that I grew up in but church activity didn't keep this feeling away from me.
I cried at night and clutch my pillow to put me to sleep. I refused to answer my phone. I had to endure the looks of *"who do you think you are now"* when I turned down men who I had slept with previously. I did all of these things so I wouldn't wake up the next morning feeling like a whore. *I want to be married again. I want to have a family. I'm just going in the wrong direction.* I went back to the meetings that I had given of myself so freely in and began to share the change that was taking place in my life. I had a few male friends who were supportive and even protective.

In January of 1995, I was helping out on the residential side of the treatment center holding meetings for residents on Wednesday nights. There I met a man named Bernie who changed the course of my life.
****

One evening in February of 1995, I went to a meeting. This meeting was special because I was celebrating 2 years of sobriety. Bernie, who no longer was a resident in the treatment program was at this meeting also. He moved up a level and now was staying in the halfway house. The meeting went well and after my time of sharing, Bernie got up, walked across the room and gave me a hug of congratulations. I felt a little uncomfortable because this was rather awkward, so I got a cup of coffee and sat down. All during the rest of the meeting, I noticed him staring at me. Some of my friends had bought balloons and a cake. After the meeting we decided to go out and eat..

Bernie met me in the hall. "Can I take your things to the car for you?"

"No thanks," I replied politely.

"Where y'all gonna eat tonight?" he continued.

"Cody's. You're more than welcome to come and continue celebratin."

We arrived at the restaurant and he came in with a young lady that he knew from the halfway house. I sat with my friends and really didn't talk to him at all, but once again I noticed him staring at me.

When everyone got ready to leave he approached my table. "Can I pay for your dinner?"

"Thank you." I said as I handed him the bill.

That night when I went home I couldn't get him off of my mind. *He's interested in me and I have to find a way to connect with him.*

The next day I remembered I had access to the phone number at the halfway house. I made the phone call and in a few minutes, he was on the other end.

"Hi this is Clare. I just wanted to thank you again for paying for my dinner last night. That was very sweet of you."

"It was my pleasure to do so," he said in a voice that was deep and husky.

Without any hesitation he asked," Clare, would you mind if I had your phone number to call you sometimes?"

"Sure." *The connection.*

"Will you save me a seat next to you tonight at the meeting?"

"Yeah, I'll see you there." I was grinning from ear to ear.

That was the beginning of another adulterous relationship. I was still married, even though I had not been with Roger for 5 years, I was legally his wife. The relationship with Bernie developed quickly. We began to date exclusively and by May he had moved into my home. I knew in my heart this man was different from any one that I had been with.

He had a good job and he was very kind to my daughter and myself. He had two children from a previous marriage and I could see that he loved them .We began to attend my church together with the kids. They came over every other weekend.

In June, the itch began to arise in me again about being married. Here I am, playing the role of a wife and a mother, which I loved, but I was not his wife.

"Bernie, I want to get married."

" I do too," he said causally.

That is as far as the conversation went.

I had begun to talk to my cousin Tanya. She was a Christian and being a Christian had become important to me. We would talk almost every day. I received a tape from her, a sermon where the preacher was talking about having sex and not being married. When we first listened to the tape we had to cut it off. It was too much truth about our situation but God was dealing with my heart.

In September, we went to a Labor Day picnic at Bernie's brother's house. After the prayer, he got everyone's attention. "Excuse me everybody, before we eat, I have an announcement to make. Clare and I are getting married."

I didn't know what to say. He had not asked me to marry him. Everyone gave their congratulations and on the way home I questioned him.

" Bernie, you never asked me to marry you."

He pulled over to the side of the rode, looked at me and said,

"Will you?"

I obtained a divorce and three months later we were wed.

Epilogue

I am not saying at all, the way Bernie and I did it was right, but that was the way it happened. The day of our wedding, we went to the altar early and asked God to forgive us for our sins and asked Him to bless our marriage.

And He did both.

There are many unnatural effects that I had to face being raised as a child in this type of environment. They were to name a few, emotional abuse, distorted thinking about sex, feelings of inadequacy, a love and hate relationship with myself, escapism through reading books, abusive men in relationships, sexual promiscuity, an inability to be faithful or keep a commitment, mistrust of men and women, abusing myself sexually, anger and high tempered, lack of respect for authority figures, alcoholism and drug abuse.

There are also many spiritual effects that followed. They were to name a few, adultery, inordinate affections, filthy language, fornication, masturbation, abortion, murder, perversions, bad dreams, sexual fantasies, pornography, insanity, rejection, bitterness, rebellion, shame, deep hurt, fear, suicide, guilt, doubt, condemnation, envy, jealousy and vain imaginations.

Yes, I was messed up and what was worse, I knew it and

couldn't do anything about it. No matter how hard I tried, I couldn't gain control. If I seemed to manage to get a handle on one thing, another thing would become evident. My life was headed in a downward tunnel and the end I saw was death.

But thanks be unto to God. He extended His love and mercy to me through His only begotten Son, Jesus Christ. God provided a way to get rid of these effects through His provision of salvation and deliverance.

It took some time for me to see the effects being removed from my life. I first had to accept God's love for me totally, no matter what I had done. I then had to forgive myself and finally forgive my parents and all those involved. Both of my parents died before I was able to forgive them in person. Through Jesus, my heart has been washed cleaned of unforgiveness towards them and all those involved.

Some of the people in this story are still alive. Some have been set free and yet others are still denying the deep seeded hurt that this one man caused.

There are no more tormenting memories. When the light exposes the darkness, the darkness has to flee.

****

Was the abuse really over?

Life is a journey.

Read: C. Lynn's **Bewitched in the Local Church**

I would like to thank everyone for reading this book.

I would appreciate your comments at www.clynn@truevine.net

The Abuser's Daughter Order Form

Use this convenient order form to order

The Abuser's Daughter

Please Print:

Name_____

Address_____

City_____

State_____

Zip Code_____

Phone_____

_____copies of book at $ 14.00 each $_____

Postage and Handling at $1.50 per book $_____

Total amount enclosed $_____

Make Checks Payable To: **Cynthia Hatcher**

Send To: **HATCHBACK Publishing**

P.O. Box 480

Genesee, Michigan 48437